Published by Smart Apple Media
1980 Lookout Drive, North Mankato, Minnesota 56003
Produced by Byron Preiss Visual Publications, Inc.

Cover design by Dean Motter
Interior design by Gilda Hannah
Edited by Howard Zimmerman

Front cover art by John Sibbick
Back cover art by Gregory S. Paul

Art Credits: Pages 1, 10, 20 © 2002 John Sibbick. Pages 3, 29 (top) © 2002
Gregory S. Paul. Pages 5, 25 © 2002 Phil Wilson. Page 7 © 2002 Christopher Srnka.
Page 8 © Berislav Krzic. Page 9 © 2002 Jan Sovak. Page 11 © 2002 Michael Carroll.
Pages 12–13, 15, 17, 19, 29 (bottom), 31 © 2002 Douglas Henderson. Pages 22–23
© 2002 Rich Penney. Page 27 © 2002 Donna Braginetz.

Printed in the U.S.A.

Library of Congress Cataloging-in-Publication Data

Olshevsky, George.
Iguanodon / by George Olshevsky and Sandy Fritz.
p. cm.—(Discovering dinosaurs)
Summary: Presents information on *Iguanodon*, including physical
characteristics, diet, habitat, known social organization, close relatives,
and areas where fossils have been found.
ISBN 1-58340-180-6
1. Iguanodon—Juvenile literature. [1. Iguanodon. 2. Dinosaurs.]
I. Fritz, Sandy. II. Title.
QE862.O65 O476 2002
567.914–dc21   2002017634

First Edition

2 4 6 8 9 7 5 3 1

IGUANODON

Sandy Fritz and George Olshevsky

SMART APPLE MEDIA

Dinosaurs lived on Earth from about 227 million to 65 million years ago. Scientists call this the Mesozoic era. It is also called the Age of Reptiles or the Age of Dinosaurs. Dinosaurs were closely related to today's reptiles and birds. In fact, many scientists now think that birds evolved from a small meat-eating dinosaur that was a swift runner. All dinosaurs were land animals. Flying reptiles (called pterosaurs) and reptiles that swam in the sea also lived during this period, but they were not dinosaurs.

The Age of Dinosaurs, the Mesozoic era, is divided into three periods. The earliest period is called the Triassic, which lasted from 248 million to 205 million years ago. Dinosaurs first appeared around the middle of this period. The Jurassic period followed, lasting from 205 million to 145 million years ago. The final period is called the Cretaceous. The Cretaceous spanned from 145 million to 65 million years ago. After the Cretaceous, dinosaurs were gone.

But during their time, dinosaurs lived everywhere on Earth, even in Antarctica. About 700 different kinds of dinosaurs have been unearthed, and many more remain in the ground awaiting discovery. There were meat-eating dinosaurs that could run fast on their long hind legs. There were four-legged, plant-eating dinosaurs 150 feet (46 m) long and weighing as much as 100 tons (91 t)! There were dinosaurs with horns, crests, and bony armor. Some dinosaurs, both meat-eaters and plant-eaters, were as small as chickens or house cats.

Everything we know about dinosaurs comes from fossils that people have dug up from the ground. Scientists examine, measure, and analyze these fossils. From them we can learn when and where dinosaurs lived. We have learned how dinosaurs walked and ran, what they hunted, and what plants they ate. We can even figure out how long they lived. Presented in this series is the most up-to-date information we have learned about dinosaurs. We hope you'll enjoy reading all about the fabulous beasts of Earth's distant past.

Meet Iguanodon

Iguanodon was an elephant-sized plant-eating dinosaur. An adult *Iguanodon* was 25 to 30 feet (7–9 m) long and probably weighed up to three tons (2.7 t). Its fossils are found mainly in Europe, where it first appeared about 140 million years ago. Its head was long and narrow, with a toothless beak at the front. Its cheek teeth were big and sturdy. The upper teeth wore against the lower teeth to keep their edges chisel-sharp. New teeth grew constantly as the old teeth wore away. On each "hand," *Iguanodon* had a large, straight "thumb" spike. It and its relatives were the only plant-eating dinosaurs that had them.

When feeding, *Iguanodon* ambled around slowly on all four legs. But when in danger, it picked up its front feet and ran away on its longer, powerful hind legs. Its tail was long and stiff. Bony rods ran the length of the tail

This page: A group of *Iguanodon* travel across an ancient shoreline. Opposite page: An *Iguanodon* stops in the middle of getting a drink of water to check for predators.

to keep it rigid. There were two possible advantages to having such a tail. Held horizontal to the ground, it provided balance for running and turning. It may also have been used to brace *Iguanodon* when the dinosaur reared up to reach tall branches for food.

The first *Iguanodon* fossils known to science were just a few bones. Their discovery in southern England was reported in 1808 by British scientist William Smith. At that time nobody knew what a dinosaur was. This was 34 years before the word "dinosaur" had even been invented. So the fossils were generally ignored.

By 1822, however, many *Iguanodon* teeth were being found by British workmen who were digging for stones to use in building. They sold the teeth to Gideon Mantell, a country doctor and fossil collector. The teeth puzzled Mantell. He spent a lot of time trying to determine what kind of animal they might have belonged to. Finally, he found teeth that matched the fossils he had. They belonged to an iguana. But the lizard's teeth were much, much smaller than the fossil teeth.

In 1825, Mantell reported that the fossil teeth had come from an extinct giant lizard. He named the animal *Iguanodon*, or "iguana tooth." After comparing the size of *Iguanodon* teeth to the teeth of an iguana, Mantell imagined that *Iguanodon* might have been a giant lizard almost 100 feet (30.4 m) long—more than three times the actual size of *Iguanodon*.

This page and opposite page: *Iguanodon* **lived in forested areas and ate from the lower branches of trees.**

This page: *Iguanodon* uses its "thumb spike" as a defensive weapon. Opposite page: The first life-size reconstruction of *Iguanodon* made it look like a reptilian rhino (top). It was nearly a century before an accurate reconstruction was done (bottom).

Iguanodon Discovered

guanodon was only the second dinosaur to be scientifically examined and named. Scientists had to try to imagine what *Iguanodon* looked like by studying its bones, without knowing much about dinosaurs. This was even more difficult because not all of its bones had been found. The first drawing of *Iguanodon* made it look like a reptilian rhinoceros. Its legs sprawled out to the sides, and its belly almost touched the ground. Its tail was long and snakelike, and dragged on the ground like a crocodile's tail.

A group of *Iguanodon* walk through a forest in search of food.

Later, scientists had more information. More *Iguanodon* and other dinosaur fossils were found. The picture of *Iguanodon* changed. It became a giant, upright, two-legged reptile. A famous painting was done of *Iguanodon* standing up tall and straight on its hind legs with its tail on the ground. It looked like the movie monster Godzilla, which was also incorrect.

Now we know that this dinosaur did not look like a reptile. *Iguanodon* walked on all four limbs but ran on its strong hind legs. Its weight was balanced over its hips, whether it was walking or running. Its body was held horizontal to the ground, and its tail was held straight out to help keep the animal balanced.

There were actually several kinds of *Iguanodon* that lived in many places throughout the world. Some of the largest have been found in Europe. Many of their fossils have been discovered in Great Britain, where the first *Iguanodon* fossils were found. A huge deposit of two dozen nearly complete *Iguanodon* skeletons was discovered in 1878. They were found by workers in a coal mine deep underground in Belgium. This discovery made *Iguanodon bernissartensis* Europe's most famous dinosaur discovery.

Iguanodon fossils have also been found in Germany, Portugal, and Spain. They have been found as far south as northern Africa, and fossilized footprints that might

***Iguanodon* walk through an area where trees have been knocked down by a storm. They are constantly on the alert for any sight, sound, or scent of danger.**

14

have been made by *Iguanodon* were discovered on some arctic islands far to the north. It seems that *Iguanodon* lived almost everywhere across Europe.

A large, heavy kind of *Iguanodon* lived in Asia. Its fossils were found by dinosaur hunters in the Gobi Desert in the late 1940s. Only some teeth and a jawbone were found, but these were enough to identify it. And in the United States, *Iguanodon* teeth, jaws, and part of a skull have been found. Although the evidence is slight, it is enough to tell us that *Iguanodon* lived in Asia and the Americas as well as Europe.

> *Iguanodon* and its relatives apparently had cheeks of some kind covering the teeth in the sides of their mouths. Although reptiles do not have cheeks, many plant-eating mammals do. Their cheeks keep plant matter from falling out of their mouths while they chew repeatedly. *Iguanodon* probably had cheeks for just this reason.

Iguanodon and Its Young

No nests or eggs belonging to *Iguanodon* have yet been found. But we do have fossil nests and eggs from a plant-eating dinosaur that was closely related to *Iguanodon*. In 1978, fossils were found in Montana from a new dinosaur that was named *Maiasaura* ("good mother lizard"). Scientists uncovered a nesting ground with fossils of *Maiasaura* nests, eggs, hatchlings, and eggshells. Because *Maiasaura* was a plant-eater similar in size and structure to *Iguanodon*, we can look at what we know about the "good mother lizard" for clues as to how *Iguanodon* lived and how it behaved.

By studying the Montana fossils, scientists found that *Maiasaura* babies had begun eating while still in the nests. This suggested that *Maiasaura* parents brought food to their young because the babies were not ready to go and find food for themselves. Their bones and muscles weren't strong enough yet. The parents probably brought food back to the nests by biting off plants, chewing, and swallowing

A young *Iguanodon* travels with its mother through the forest in search of food.

them. Back at the nest, they would bring the half-digested food back up so the babies could feed on it. *Iguanodon* probably fed its young the same way. *Maiasaura* and *Iguanodon* probably continued to care for their young for several years, teaching them which plants were best to eat and what dangers to avoid.

The *Maiasaura* fossils discovered in Montana have told us many things about *Iguanodon* and related plant-eating dinosaurs. Scientists found that the dinosaurs were in seven different size groups. The smallest was a hatchling, a newborn *Maiasaura*. The largest was a full-grown adult. If babies were hatched about a year apart, then it may have taken *Maiasaura* seven years to become a fully grown dinosaur.

If it was like *Maiasaura*, then *Iguanodon* started life very small. *Maiasaura* babies were less than a foot (30 cm) long when they hatched. In the seven years it took to become an adult, they grew quickly. *Maiasaura* babies had short faces with big eyes. As they grew, their faces became longer, their beaks grew harder, and the number of rows of teeth in their jaws became greater.

Scientists think *Maiasaura* could have lived for another 40 to 50 years after reaching full size. As noted earlier, an adult *Iguanodon* could have been up to 30 feet (9 m) long and weighed as much as three tons (2.7 t). After reaching this size, it, like *Maiasaura*, probably lived to be 40 or 50 years old, if it didn't get eaten first.

What Iguanodon Ate

We can tell by looking at its teeth that *Iguanodon* was not a meat-eater. Meat-eaters have teeth like knives, made for slicing through muscle and bone. *Iguanodon* had a beak for cropping off plant matter, and rows of squat teeth made

This painting is based on a fossilized set of footprints, called a trackway. The trackway was discovered in New Mexico, and showed the prints of three dinosaurs quite similar to *Iguanodon* walking.

for grinding it up. The dominant plants when *Iguanodon* was alive were related to today's pine trees. *Iguanodon* probably fed mainly on these.

Plants are made from a tough fiber called cellulose. It is hard to digest. Birds, which cannot chew, often swallow small stones to help grind up the seeds they eat. We know that many plant-eating dinosaurs also swallowed stones to help break up plants because their fossils have been found with these polished stones in the area where their stomachs would have been. Scientists think that *Iguanodon* also might have swallowed stones for this purpose, although "stomach stones" have not yet been found with its fossils.

Iguanodon's Social Life

We think that *Iguanodon* lived and traveled in herds as many other plant-eating animals do. About 250 years ago, great herds of buffalo roamed the American plains. We know this because it was recent enough for people to have kept records of it. But for a dinosaur that lived 140 million years ago, the records are scarce.

One record of dinosaur herding is trackways. These are sets of footprints that have turned to stone over time. Many trackways have been found that show dinosaurs of the same kind moving in the same direction. However, it cannot be determined if they were all moving together in a group or if the tracks were made at the same time. If they were, this is evidence for herding.

The discovery of two dozen *Iguanodon* skeletons in a coal mine in Belgium led some scientists to think they were all part of a herd

This page: The remarkable "hand" of *Iguanodon*. Opposite page: A mother *Iguanodon* walks on all four limbs, while her baby walks on two. *Iguanodon* was capable of doing both.

A herd of *Iguanodon* tries to
slip past a drinking predator,
but it has caught their scent.

that died together. But we will never know for sure. The dinosaurs could have died in the same place but at different times.

We do know for certain that *Iguanodon*'s close relative lived in herds. The fossil bone beds of *Maiasaura* in Montana spread for several square miles and hold the fossils of as many as 10,000 *Maiasaura*. And if *Maiasaura* lived and traveled in herds, it's quite likely that *Iguanodon* did, too.

Remarkable Hands

The "hands" of *Iguanodon* were curiously built, and the dinosaur apparently used them in several different ways. The first digit, or "thumb," was a long, thick, sharp spike. *Iguanodon* probably used it for defense and perhaps in battles during the mating season. It could surely have inflicted a painful wound on an attacking predator.

The fifth digit, or "pinky," was long and flexible. It had no claw or spike on the end. It was opposed to the rest of the hand, much like our thumbs. This means it could have allowed the hand to grasp objects. This may have helped the dinosaur to strip leaves from tree branches.

The second, third, and fourth digits were very stout, and the second and third ended in thick, broad nails that looked like hooves. Many plant-eating mammals, such as horses, cows, and sheep, have hooves. The hooves supported *Iguanodon* when it walked on all four feet. Fossil footprints made by *Iguanodon* show that the dinosaur

Another large predator that might have hunted *Iguanodon* is *Neovenator*. This meat-eater was 26 feet (8 m) long, almost the same size as a fully grown *Iguanodon*. It was similar to the North American predator *Allosaurus*.

used all four limbs for walking, though it could also run on its two hind legs.

It is remarkable that *Iguanodon*'s hands had so many uses. The big plant-eater used them for walking, grasping objects, eating, and defending itself.

Who Ate Iguanodon?

It seems logical that bigger animals eat smaller ones, but that's not always what happens. An adult *Iguanodon* would have been a whopper of a meal for any meat-eater, but not many huge predators lived in the same time and place as *Iguanodon*. It may have been smaller animals that hunted and ate this three-ton (2.7 t) plant-eater.

In Europe, there were two smaller predators that could have attacked *Iguanodon* youngsters and babies. One was called *Eotyrannus*. It was 15 feet (5 m) long and weighed about 500 pounds (230 kg). Scientists think it may have been an early relative of the great *Tyrannosaurus rex*.

The other predator was larger than *Eotyrannus*. It was about 30 feet (9 m) long and had a massive snout filled with dagger-sharp teeth. It was named *Baryonyx*, which means "heavy claw." This refers to the sharp, curved, foot-long (30 cm) claw it had on each hand. We know that *Baryonyx* ate fish, because fossilized fish scales have been found in the stomach of one *Baryonyx* fossil. But it may have hunted and eaten young *Iguanodon*, too.

In western North America, *Iguanodon* probably shared its range with *Utahraptor*. *Utahraptor* was one of the largest of a group of meat-eating dinosaurs that probably fed on plant-eaters larger than themselves. It was about 20 feet (6 m) in length, and the

A *Utahraptor* pair on the prowl. These large raptors could hunt, chase, and kill a full-grown *Iguanodon*.

sharp, curved claws on its feet were each a foot (30 cm) long. All raptors had one large, nasty curved claw on each foot. As the raptors walked, their "killing claws" would rarely have touched the ground. These claws were weapons, and walking on them would have dulled their points.

Raptors were smart, and they had good eyesight. Scientists think they probably hunted their prey in packs, like modern wolves. Working together, a pack of raptors could have brought down an adult *Iguanodon*.

Traveling in herds may have been a way for *Iguanodon* to protect itself. A single adult *Iguanodon* wouldn't have stood a chance if it was attacked by a *Utahraptor* pack. Even if it used its thumb spikes in defense, no *Iguanodon* could have fought them off. These predators were the kings of their world.

The End of Iguanodon

More than 90 percent of all the animal species that have ever lived on Earth are now extinct. Some species become extinct from sudden catastrophes, such as an asteriod smashing into the earth, or a giant volcanic explosion. A giant asteroid did smash into the earth at the end of the Age of Dinosaurs, and was probably responsible for their extinction. But *Iguanodon* was gone long before the end of the Age of Dinosaurs. Most dinosaurs became extinct for reasons that are not well understood. After all, a dinosaur such as *Iguanodon* was quite successful. It spread across the world, and branched into several different species. It's hard to see why it would have died out.

No known catastrophe occurred when the last *Iguanodon* met its end. Its extinction could have been the result of disease. Or it

Opposite page, top: A trio of plant-eating heterodontosaurs. These ancestors of *Iguanodon* were smaller and weighed less. Bottom: After *Iguanodon* disappeared, its descendants, such as these three duck-billed *Kritosaurus*, took their place. These hadrosaurs were larger than *Iguanodon*.

could have been caused by a change in the plant food that was available. The plants that covered the earth when *Iguanodon* first appeared were replaced over time by new plants that had tougher stems and leaves, and trees with tougher bark. Perhaps *Iguanodon* simply couldn't adapt to these changes. However it happened, the fossil record shows that *Iguanodon* lived for about 20 million years, and then suddenly it was gone.

Hadrosaurs were the descendants of the iguanodontids. They are often called "duck-billed" dinosaurs because the front of a hadrosaur's snout was flat and broad like the bill of a duck. This "duck bill" supported a thick, horny beak. It helped the dinosaur bite off the juiciest parts of the plants it ate. The beak of *Iguanodon* was already broadened and thickened, but it was developed even further in the hadrosaurs. Hadrosaurs were built like iguanodon-tids, but they were generally larger and heavier and had longer limbs. Many hadrosaurs had bony head crests. Each different hadrosaur species had a different kind of crest.

Hadrosaurs are famous for having had more teeth in their jaws than any other dinosaur. An adult hadrosaur could have had more than 1,000 teeth at any given time. Not all of these teeth were in use; most of them were there to replace the teeth above or below as they wore away. Each tooth in use may have had six or seven teeth under and alongside it, waiting their turn. *Iguanodon* had only one or two replacement teeth in position. Having so many replacement teeth growing and ready to go helped these plant-eaters chew tougher plants than an *Iguanodon* could. Hadrosaurs were probably better able to consume the new plants and trees that took over around the time that *Iguanodon* disappeared.

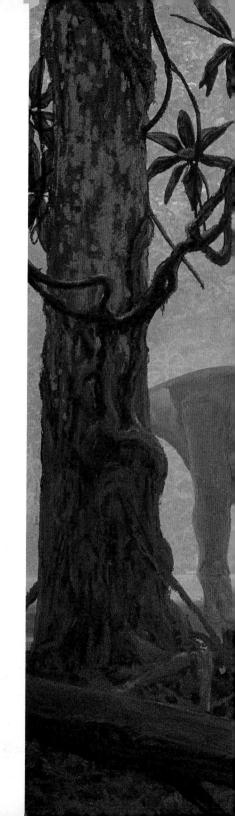

Many hadrosaurs, such as these *Corythosaurus*, had bony head crests.

GLOSSARY

Allosaurus (AL-uh-SAWR-us): an allosaurid. The most fearsome predator of the Jurassic period.

Baryonyx (BAR-ee-ON-iks): a meat-eating dinosaur with enormous claws and a crocodile-like head.

cellulose (SELL-you-los): tough fiber of which plants are made.

Corythosaurus (kor-ITH-uh-SAWR-us): a hadrosaur named for its crested skull.

digit (DIJ-it): a finger or toe.

Eotyrannus (EE-oh-tih-RAN-us): an ancestor of *T. rex*, about one-third the size.

extinct (ik-STINKT): no longer existing.

fossil (FAH-sill): a remnant of a living organism that has turned to stone over time.

hadrosaurs (HAD-ruh-sawrz): the "duck-billed" dinosaurs.

hatchling (HACH-ling): any animal just born from an egg.

heterodontosaurs (HET-er-oh-DON-toe-sawrz): plant-eating dinosaurs that were ancestors of *Iguanodon*.

Iguanodon (ih-GWAN-uh-don): a plant-eating dinosaur with thumb spikes on its "hands."

Iguanodon bernissartensis (ih-GWAN-uh-don BER-nis-are-TEN-sis): one kind of *Iguanodon* discovered in Bernissart, Belgium.

iguanodontids (ih-gwan-uh-DON-tidz): belonging to the *Iguanodon* family of plant-eating dinosaurs.

kritosaurus (KRIT-o-SAWR-US): a "duck-billed" dinosaur.

Maiasaura (MY-uh-SAWR-uh): a hadrosaurid. The name means "good mother lizard."

Neovenator (NEE-oh-VEN-uh-tor): a meat-eating dinosaur similar to *Allosaurus*.

predator (PRED-uh-tor): an animal that hunts and eats other animals for food.

prey (pray): any animal that is hunted as food.

pterosaurs (TERR-uh-sawrz): flying reptiles from the Mesozoic era.

trackways (TRAK-wayz): footprints left in the mud that have changed to stone over a long time.

Tyrannosaurus rex (tie-RAN-uh-SAWR-us REX): a tyrannosaurid. One of the largest meat-eaters that ever lived.

Utahraptor (YOO-tah-RAP-tor): a meat-eating dinosaur with a long, curved claw on each foot.

INDEX